# Dear Future

poems by
Nina Corwin

Glass Lyre Press

Copyright © 2017 Nina Corwin
Paperback ISBN: 978-1-941783-35-1

All rights reserved: except for the purpose of quoting brief passages for review, no part of this book may be reproduced or transmitted in any form or by any means, electronic or mechanical, including photocopying, recording, or by any information storage and retrieval system, without permission in writing from the publisher.

Cover art: © Bliksem Steen
Author photo: Bill Harrison
Design & layout: Steven Asmussen
Copyediting: Linda E. Kim

Glass Lyre Press, LLC
P.O. Box 2693
Glenview, IL 60025
www.GlassLyrePress.com

# Contents

| | |
|---|---|
| Poem In Which I Go To the Movies and See My Future In the Previews | 5 |
| Darwin's Telescope | 7 |
| Poem With a Line From an Ad for Capital One | 8 |
| Sal(i)vation | 9 |
| Tips For Today's Commodities Watcher | 11 |
| simultaneous equations #2 | 12 |
| Invitation | 15 |
| Interior With Artificial Leaves | 17 |
| Stuck | 19 |
| When It Rains, It Rains | 20 |
| What to Pack For the Apocalypse | 21 |
| In Due Time | 22 |
| | |
| Acknowledgements | 27 |
| About the Author | 29 |

# Poem In Which I Go To the Movies and See My Future In the Previews

The clip starts with piles of dishes
the present left for the future
to scrub, a novice jockey
fretting before his maiden race.

The release is due any day.

My future is a dart board, a moon
with a rocket in its eye. It occupies itself
clipping coupons and spinning

straw into gold. The soy beans of my future
aren't worth the dirt they sprouted from.

My future finds a time
machine with a rusty telegraph inside,
tries to send a message back but can't
get its lips to sync.

When I get there, my future meets me
at the door apologizing for the disarray.
Sings *Don't Blame Me* in the key of B flat.

The writers are calling
my future *Junior* —

Junior warming up in the bull pen.
Pouring through Ripley's
Believe it or Not. Junior looking for a date
to the matinée. Junior Unbound.

From here, it looks like Junior's canoe
has rounded the bend. There's a roar
up ahead. It's the MGM lion
with today's feature.

# Darwin's Telescope

In a carved-up corner of the Amazon, an old gardener keeps her cabbages and cucumbers apart. Shaking her head, she explains – they will kill each other if given the chance.

A panel of scientists votes to strip Pluto of planetary status. The grumbling opposition asks: how round is round?

In second grade, my best friend makes me clean her room. Alleging friends in nether places, she threatens to hex me if I refuse.

Pretty soon, belief becomes suspension bridge.

Not long after, I take Underdog, with his little white U and blue cartoon cape, to be my psychic savior. In private, I stick pins in Polly Purebred's voodoo likeness.

Teeth bared, a pair of dogs grapples for the single bone between them. The victor marks the hydrant of his choice.

Bullies of every stripe and paw print swagger through the ecosystem. The sniveling little guy bellies up.

I, too, have my hungers. The hunter-gatherer in me. The need to name on the table of my tongue. The need the need the need.

Every week, another contestant is voted off the island. Implanted at the base of my brain, my survivalist microchip is ticking.

# POEM WITH A LINE FROM AN AD FOR CAPITAL ONE

The future is standing in the middle
of Macy's and can't find it's way out.

On the mezzanine, a maze
of silk ties arrange themselves by hue and design.

According to the voice above,
a sales associate is needed in cosmetics.

*Is anybody there?*

I want a gold watch but there's no one to pay.
I want an afternoon of splurge and beauty.

Beyond that, who knows where
satisfaction lies?

Perhaps a little something in black. Organza. Size 5.

Consider something for nothing
down. Here's something cozy at a flexible rate.
Something the children will never grow out of.

The future needs to know: Will it shrink in the wash?

There's nobody passing out answers. Just layers
of makeup and artful packaging.

That's what you get
from retail. Someone who can sell a hat
pin to a red balloon. Talk a sock
monkey out of its socks.

*What's in your wallet?* they inquire.
The future is looking for a sign.

# Sal(i)vation

The chief of neurology knocks
back a glass of water and all of us
swallow in synchrony. A signal

your Insula gets the message,
he explains. Mine keeps firing off memos.
Attention: Pavlov. Attention: Mammary.

Wherever I turn, hungry dogs,
shivering birds, lilies wilting
in the dark.

There are two faces
to survival. Yours and mine.
See: we have mirrors in our eyes.

Not far off: compassion lies
sandwiched between
upper crust and lower.

*Feed Me* cries an orphanage
and somewhere a mother
becomes milk.

Who among us couldn't use a sip?
*Me First* the voices pitch
from the gallery.

We are ushered into a room full
of students paid to push buttons.
Those on the other side are shocked.

Where do you sit?

Let's play planet and moon. Take turns
in each other's orbit. Look at me.
Hello.   Hello.

I have two loaves of bread.
A thimble of something to wash it down.
Dinner's almost ready.

# TIPS FOR TODAY'S COMMODITIES WATCHER

Recent fluctuations notwithstanding,
the boom has overlooked the fruit.

Cotton is perched on a catapult.
It's got that lean and hungry look.

From here to China, glut has turned
to shortage. Bargains lurk in the bales.

To say hot commodity is to fill your mouth
with coal and shit diamonds.

Beyond our wildest hopes, Goldilocks
has assumed the position, setting off

a chain reaction in silk stockings.
Apprehension is to be expected

when approaching the curves. Hold on.
In the orchards, yellow jackets are swarming.

Yesterday's barons of white gold are gone,
fallen from their antebellum trees.

Slick polyester's passé –
an overpriced and sweaty substitute.

Don't be fooled by apparent inversions.
When in doubt, remember to check your pulse.

Egged on by a market in heat, bullish
heads are starting to spin. The verge is in

the offing, my friends. Cotton is again
the pick. This is the time to jump.

## SIMULTANEOUS EQUATIONS #2

perhaps I hatched
full blown
from a thought balloon.　　　*o jaundiced sun asunder*
emerging solo　　　　　　　　*bleeding yolk*
from a cell split open.
shimmied down
a strand of after-
birth. pop!
goes the postulate.
that was it. I hid
beneath a bush
and shielded my eyes.
today I put aside my pen　　　*o vein of mine*
and ruler,　　　　　　　　　　*dripped dry*
stymied. thought
instead to pan
for gold in the eureka
moment, when a sudden flood
of watershed came gushing
and I floundered.
so long
I've lived a life
of transitives: of scratch-
mark pigeons
signifying in the dark.　　　　*come bloody gold*
where all I culled　　　　　　*from stingy river*
was bait
and switch. rude slurry
of rudiments –

not much
substance but
I'd eat
the meal served
me, meeting each *as bones in a sandbox*
and every inch *half buried & questioning breath*
of offered worm
with beak stretched
wide. I'd
slurp hypotheses
for breakfast
(some half-baked,
the rest refried).
until last week
there came a theorem: *where faith is to freefall*
solve for X. *as morsel to endless intestine*
I tried.
but reaped no equals
from the formulaic
files in my cupboard
of assumptions.
how did I arrive
at this *twisted middle passage*
uneasy juncture? *swamped in paradox*
and how
shall I dismount?
no answer comes
from any ether
only permutations

of the possible.
those that sprout           *in double negatives*
from stumps            *with square roots barren*
and those with wings
that light
on window ledges,
grin at me
and chirp:
if hope is hatched,         *(before two unsolved eyes)*
from where? and how?    *& by what measure?*

# Invitation

The girl in the bleachers tells
the bashful athlete he should never
wear a shirt.
This makes his washboard muscles smile.
He enters the memory
into a matrix of gratefuls.

A stuttering child remarks,
"You l-l-look hungry, Miss P-p-pigeon."
and scatters a handful of popcorn.
Ten minutes later,
a man in a coma wakes
up and tells his nurses a joke.

Every time a car pulls over
to offer a lift, it's a prince
charming moment, a gift of
I-love-you. Stick out your thumb,
there's a plum on its way. Just
when it seems as if summer forgot.

You can see the morning
glories straining at their stakes, heads full
of thirst. Water hydrants, untapped,
wait to be needed. Look –
incipient windows open to anything;
curtains fluttering as only curtains can.

From opposite sides of the street, two
dogs yap and yap. Herds of traffic surge
between. The animals
tug at their leashes, tails wagging.
How could the owners help
but notice?

Imagine: snatches of piano
in a major key –
at least more major than minor.
It's not so far a stretch:
Hand out, smudged
envelope, sunlight inside.

# INTERIOR WITH ARTIFICIAL LEAVES

What I meant to say, but the crop of false fruit kept intruding, is that doorbells are not destiny. They have no teeth. Split infinities while waiting for a ring.

When you come, you come without warning labels or guarantees (black box from a bastion of caveat emptor). All I ask is the insider's peek.

---

The leaves have a theme song. It's inspired by all those lullabies with falling babies and broken branches. I'll sing you a snatch before the future explodes our foregone conclusion:

The heart is a minefield awaiting its moment. It bruises when served open-faced. Parentheticals wipe their feet on every act of contrition. Above the sink, a cylinder of light winks like it's in on the deal.

---

I got a call last month from a woman who uncorked a bottle of noxious recollections. She asked if I could put them back.

I tried to tell her there's always a stain that won't scrub, but my tongue became a fountain spouting wishful thoughts. After that, I planted my spleen beneath the bed to see if anything would grow.

Now, my duct work is choking with vines, woodpeckers hit their heads against a concrete tree. Rakes are no match for the mess that spreads between us.

---

I have a dangling proposition: part apostle in the garden, part storm in your escape route. A dim bulb's hope for harvesting sunrise from shrapnel and sawdust –

Let's say we blow up the second act and spatter gold paint on what's left. Send hope to the front lines to mop up the spills while we sleep.

# Stuck

There are cattle prods everywhere.
Cattle prods & carrots. Playing
their parts. I know, I've seen them.

Heard the freight cars rattle
with echoes of empty. French kiss
of the mantis. Nothing to stop it.

I have witnessed the cunning
duet of lure & hook. The catch, all
flesh and scales. I've calculated

entries & exits. The number of keys:
who keeps them; which side the lock takes.
Check the math if you don't believe me.

There's something ancient playing
in the theater of spider & fly. What makes
a sticky situation, for starters.

*Look.* What's that
up ahead? Some sort of shed,
stink of livestock, corrugated ramp –

*Hey wait! Quit pushing me.*

# When It Rains, It Rains

The cloud bank has been drained. Cashed
out. Robbed of mirages. Gone
the snail, the rabbit, the whole flock of sheep.

If there's a silver lining, I can't find it.
Maybe it followed. Maybe it's wherever
Tinkerbell's shadow got off

to — run like nylons from a calloused heel.
Or I'm the bloody heel the shadow left
behind. It's me I miss

and I don't know what
I'm looking for. Nothing but a maybe
hand shaking a silvery bell.

I look under the bed and there
is someone's father swallowed by vodka
bottles, trees with Xes chalkmarked for chopping.

On the block, the man's left
a note pleading *don't*
*the sycamores count for anything?* I've looked

under S – found a dozen synonyms for *should*.
Found stick figures, staple guns, an orphaned shoe.
I've paged through the catalogue of after-

thoughts: p.s. pig slops and postage stamps.
Maybe I heard it wrong. Maybe it's a silk
lining that's given me the slip.

Could be it's run off to find itself
a place along the midway in the bright,
bright circus of the future.

## What to Pack For the Apocalypse

A faceless man runs down a pitched roof,
gladiators at his back. The dreamer wakes in free fall.

A little help from erosion and the precipice approaches
at the buzz rate of killer bees.

When heads of state play chicken
on a cliff, the speed of the hotrod is everybody's business.

What we have here is more than a failure to communicate
or a sloppy lot of rowdies butting heads in a mosh pit.

If the life boat leaks, what to pack for the apocalypse
(iPad, change purse, teddy bear) is *not* the operative question.

A father-to-be boards a jet, suitcase bulging with worries.
At crusing altitude, he opens his tray table and the plane flips

upside down. Outside the window, a banner flaps.
Quit fussing, it says, you're going one way or another.

# In Due Time

1.
Dear Future, call me
a miserable speck of your past.
But there are throngs of us

here. Some who mumble
when they pray, some plotting
data points, others who cast lots

to see
who will go first.
Can you give us a hint?

2.
Dear Future, day comes with its cross-
haired sun; night with its carousel of stars:
the shooters, the burn outs, the burning

still. Is there any order to this?
Even the chicken and egg agree
to disagree.

Our steps are bedeviled
with questions: What
will we be

when we grow up? Will we walk
through a door or fall
off the edge?

3.
Dear Future, I can see
the bull in you snorting and kicking
up dirt. An ant afraid to be stomped.

And I worry. Like a farmer
with a finger in the air, or parents
checking car seats and nanny-cams.

I see rabbits swollen with brood,
you in the breach, twisted
cord around your neck.

If I could, I'd send a midwife
but I haven't got your address.

4.
The future dearly wants to tell us:

Economists are no better
than weathermen. Too much
growth saps the bones.

There's an omen
in every phenomenon.
The edge is near.

The future turns
to Moses. Holy, holy.
But the prophet's tongue is tied.

So it pulls Chicken Little aside. To spread
the word. But the bird thinks she's dreaming
so the warnings won't come out.

5.
Dear Future, I hear you
at the trough, gagging on our pig-
eyed inventions, our noxious droppings.

If I could, I'd fix you
the feast you deserve.
I would. Spare no expense

on the latest vaccine.
But there are no pennies
to pick up. I'm sorry.

6.
At sunrise, we set
out on a journey, aging as we go.
Our caravan makes for that place

where parallels meet. An old moon
waves on a bridge
of sighs.

From the dash, a bass vibration
comes. A ringtone of milk spilling.
It's the future on the line.

# Acknowledgements

Grateful acknowledgment is made to the editors of the following journals where these poems or versions of these poems first appeared:

*DMQ Review*
    In Due Time
    When It Rains, It Rains

*Drunken Boat*
    Simultaneous Equations #2

*Fifth Wednesday Journal*
    Poem in Which I Go to the Movies
        and See My Future in the Previews

*Hotel Amerika*
    Tips for Today's Commodities Watcher

*Harvard Review*
    What to Pack for the Apocalypse

*Kettle Blue*
    Poem with a Line From an Ad for Capital One

*Parthenon West*
    Darwin's Telescope

*RHINO*
    Invitation
    Sal(i)vation

*Verse*
    Interior With Artificial Leaves

Thanks to *From the Fishouse:* an online audio archive of emerging poets, www.fishousepoems.org for archiving recordings of the following poems on the Web:

"Interior With Artificial Leaves" and "Natural Selection" (now "Darwin's Telescope."

I would like to thank the following teachers and writers for the guidance, friendship, and wisdom that nurtured this poet and her poems into present form: Heather McHugh, Ravi Shankar, Cyrus Cassels, Ralph Hamilton, Bill Yarrow, Al DeGenova, Larry Janowski. And my love and gratitude to my first reader, husband and best friend Bill Harrison.

# About the Author

**Nina Corwin** is the author of two books of poetry, *The Uncertainty of Maps* and *Conversations With Friendly Demons and Tainted Saints.* Her poetry has been nominated for the Pushcart Prize and has appeared in *Harvard Review, From the Fishouse, Drunken Boat, Forklift OH, Hotel Amerika, New Ohio Review/nor, Poetry East, Southern Poetry Review* and *Verse.* Corwin is an Advisory Editor for *Fifth Wednesday Journal* and curator for the literary series at Chicago's Woman Made Gallery. In daylight hours, she is a practicing psychotherapist known for her work on behalf of victims of violence.

# Glass Lyre Press

exceptional works to replenish the spirit

Glass Lyre Press is an independent literary publisher interested in technically accomplished, stylistically distinct, and original work. Glass Lyre seeks diverse writers that possess a dynamic aesthetic and an ability to emotionally and intellectually engage a wide audience of readers.

Glass Lyre's vision is to connect the world through language and art. We hope to expand the scope of poetry and short fiction for the general reader through exceptionally well-written books, which evoke emotion, provide insight, and resonate with the human spirit.

Poetry Collections
Poetry Chapbooks
Select Short & Flash Fiction
Anthologies

www.GlassLyrePress.com

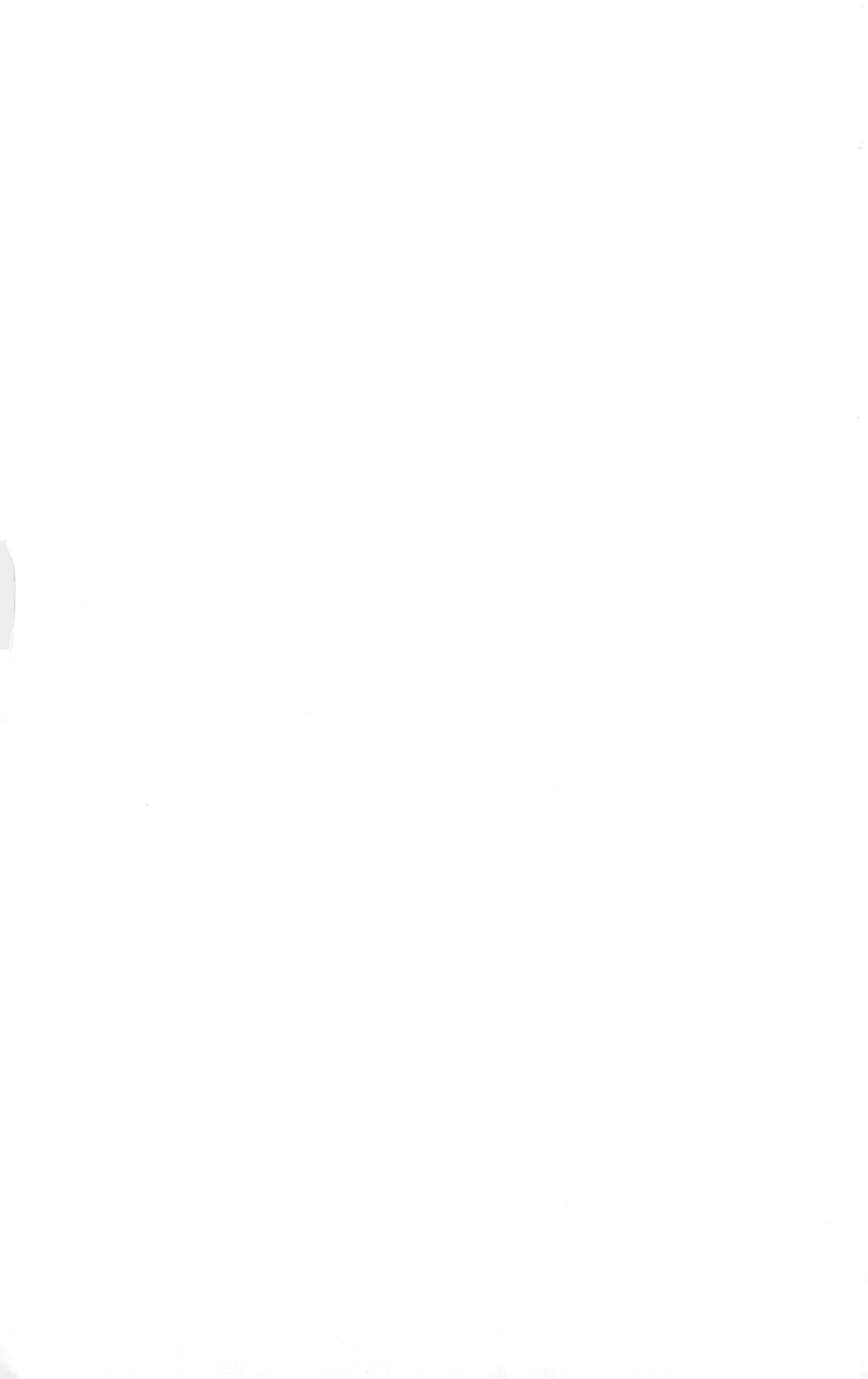

CPSIA information can be obtained
at www.ICGtesting.com
Printed in the USA
BVHW090348291022
650587BV00002B/8